M000190585

THE

DEMONIZATION

OF

MENTAL

ILLNESS

Dr. Donna M. Scott

Demonization of Mental Illness

All Scripture taken from the New King James Version® unless otherwise noted. Copyright © 1982 by Thomas Nelson. Used by permission. All rights reserved.

Scripture taken from the New King James Version®. Copyright © 1982 by Thomas Nelson. Used by permission. All rights reserved.

The Authorized (King James) Version of the Bible ('the KJV'), the rights in which are vested in the Crown in the United Kingdom, is reproduced here by permission of the Crown's patentee, Cambridge University Press.

Copyright © 2016 Donna Maria Scott
P.O. Box 1945
Muncie, IN 47308
www.lordsimage.com
All rights reserved.

ISBN-10: 0-9984160-0-2
ISBN-13: 978-0-9984160-0-7

Front cover picture of Auvon Chandler by Kizmin Jones

DEDICATION

Dedicated to

Jeffrey, Jazmin, Kandace, Khalil, Keyonis and Tra'Vion

~ Auntie Donna loves you!

In loving memory of Jeffrey, Flynt and Terrell

TABLE OF CONTENTS

Foreword

Would you like to know the difference between mental illness and demonic possession? Are you aware of the stigmas associated with these conditions, especially in the religious community? Do you know about the forlorn plight of the victims who are plagued by these conditions, due to the lack of sensitivity to them, and the efforts that need to be made in order to reduce the illnesses' stigmatization that exists in the church, the community and the world at large?

In her book, ***Demonization of Mental Illness***, Dr. Donna Maria Scott answers these questions and more with a new and refreshing look at the topic of mental illness versus demonic possession. She eloquently discusses the distinctions between the two conditions with an erudite excellence that elucidates the deep-rooted obscurities that have rendered the topic(s) borderline taboo. She provides welcomed insight into the myriad of challenges with which victims, health care providers, the religious community and faith-based organizations, and other entities are faced in addressing the issues of properly dealing with such a poignant topic.

Dr. Scott gives the reader a plethora of examples of mental illness versus "illnesses" associated with demonic possession. She supports her findings and conclusive arguments by providing relevant and timely statistics, and by citing infallible biblical, journal, and industry-expert writings. Her in-depth research into the topic has allowed her to bring to light much information that historically has been obscured, unaddressed or simply ignored.

Particularly in the religious community, mental illness and demonic possession have been inter-related and many times surmised to be one and the same. Dr. Scott's work will enlighten the readers' perspectives and provide a heightened awareness of the fallacy of this perception. Some of the interesting topics that she takes an in-depth look at include: how the church approaches mental illness, how the Bible views infirmities, mental illness in the criminal justice system, and methods and modalities of hope for victims of mental illness and demonic possession.

In my professional work as a Behavioral Counselor, an instructor in an urban non-profit organization, and a pastor of a growing congregation, I have encountered many people who have been beleaguered by illnesses that I ignorantly misjudged. Early in my career, I had clients who displayed behavior that led me to believe that they were demon possessed, but were in actuality mentally ill, simply needing to take their medication. Upon doing so, the erratic behavior changed substantially, for the better. I have also witnessed people who have behaved in ways that I interpreted as mental illness, but were actually plagued by demonic influences. In those days, if I had read Dr. Donna Scott's book, no doubt I would have approached many of those situations differently, with more expertise, and certainly with more confidence that I was giving the proper treatment for the proper illness.

Dr. Donna Scott's book, ***The Demonization of***

Mental Illness, will provide the reader with much (and in many cases, new) insight on the subject of mental illness versus demonic possession, how to distinguish between the two conditions, and veritable ways to competently address each one for the betterment of the client/patient/victim. For members of the clergy, laity, health professions, and any other societal segment that is faced with the challenges of providing proper care and assistance to people who battle mental illness or the spirits of demonic possession, this book is a must read!

Sharon L Johnson, Ph.D.
Pastor, President/CEO,
Healing Waters Ministries, Inc.
Saint Louis, Missouri

Preface

The idea of prejudice and stigmatization in the church is as unthinkable as a fish living in the dessert. The very foundation of the organism we call church breaths acceptance and unconditional love. This is the reason I found the absence of information, resources and ministry surrounding mental health to be contradictory to the tenets of faith. How could the God of Glory be remiss in addressing this area specifically when the very essence of humanity and the circumstances of life promote such profound complexities that often lead one to experience various levels of hopelessness?

This book is an in-depth look at the phenomenon known as mental illness in view of the biblical principle often referred to as "wholeness". It is virtually impossible to teach a Holistic message without including the mental health of an individual. The exhortation throughout biblical scripture, encourages a person of faith to seek wholeness in body, soul and spirit. Eliminating any part of the trichotomy of humanity opens opportunity for fallacy to attack faith. More importantly, the desire of God to be glorified is relevant even to the existence of mental illness; after all He did come to heal ALL manner of sicknesses and diseases. If it exists, God is available to heal it, no exclusions! So why does the stigmatization of mental illness continue its cruel manipulation, even in our churches? I believe it lives in the lack of information, education and resources. This book seeks to eliminate the myths by addressing the facts and exposing the spiritual misconceptions that forces parishioners everywhere to *suffer in silence*.

As what the mental health community call a "suicide survivor", "survivor of suicide" and an ordained minister of the Pentecostal persuasion, I have experienced the darkness and isolation associated with a "believer" diagnosed with clinical depression and suicidal ideation. Suffering from the residue of losing my own biological brother to suicide, which resulted in my own depression, I found it more than difficult to find the help and empathy I desperately sought in the place I so deeply loved, THE CHURCH. I now understand that most of the absence of help was due to lack of understanding, education and information. The religion of church offered the only explanation plausible, which in most cases in situations similar to my own, was attributed to demonic possession and could only be addressed with the ascribed procedure for demon elimination. This approach alone has furthered the stigmatization of mental illness and delayed healing for thousands suffering with a plethora of diagnosed mental illnesses. While this book will give full credence to the manifestations of demonic activity, we will also examine the need to be able to discern when abnormal activity is a result of something physiological.

My love for the church and the people God demands this book in this time. It is important that those with a diagnosis of a clinical mental illness have the same hope in the healing power of God that a person diagnosed with cancer or any other medical disease that humanity faces in light of a sinful world. What full service hospital would eliminate a mental health ward? Likewise, if a hospital is the analogy of the church, then by all means it is time we arm ourselves with relevance to address the ailments of ALL mankind. This book is the answer that every

Pastor and leader has been searching for to better serve the souls that have been placed in their loving care. May God bless you all and grant you courage and knowledge to address this unique area of ministry.

Acknowledgements

First and foremost, to Jesus the Christ, Son of the living God who died for my sins and loved me enough BEFORE the foundations of the earth, to fill me with the Precious Gift of the Holy Ghost, which is the enabling power in my life every day. Without the constant reminder in my spirit thru the Holy Spirit, the completion of this book would not have been possible.

To my spiritual coverings Apostle Larry J. Baylor (Lady Tanika) and Elder Marlon T. Baylor (Lady Ida), I love and appreciate you so very much! I am thoroughly convinced that any spiritual success I am experiencing at this time is directly contributed to the anointing on the lives of my leaders. Thank you for imparting Kingdom principles into my life and releasing me to operate in the governmental office God intended for me from the foundation of the world. Thank you for EVERY word of encouragement which allowed to move beyond those areas of stagnation. I am FOREVER grateful and humbled to work under the ministry of such Generals in the Kingdom!

Thank you to Queen Twyla for declaring verbally the thing God wanted to do in my life. I owe you so much love for pulling my doctorate degree out of me, which launched the commencement of this book.

A special acknowledgement goes out to the Mothers in Zion that poured so richly into my life, Evangelist I.C. Bonner (deceased), Evangelist Sallie Jefferson and Minister Maxine Moore. I love them all for the patience and the wisdom of God that was so freely given.

A special thank you to my biological Sister, Pamela, who encouraged me to complete this project in ways she will never understand. Losing your only son and watching you sorrow was difficult, but your willingness to stop grieving to make sure you supported me is one of the most selfless things I have experienced, second only to God's sacrifice of His Son. Love you Sister/Daughter more and more!!!

To my Mother, Juanita, my Sister, Tracie and my entire family who mean so very much to me and remain the motivation to succeed in all areas of my life.

Lastly, to my Faith Miracle Temple church family. So many of you have spoken such encouragement into my life, I could never list all the names. Know that I realize my strength is in the multitude and I could have never accomplished this project alone.

Introduction

The following chapters will serve to research and address the level of stigmatization and demonization of mental illness within the religious community. By examining statistical information surrounding, health, mental health and access to care, the facts will expose the emergency in implementing sound ministry in both the areas of prevention and intervention. This book will show the biblical anecdotes and doctrinal teachings that support the compassionate approach needed to assist suffering individuals on their journey.

The residue of losing a sibling to suicide and experiencing the religious community's response to his death, ignited the need to expose ignorance of mental illness and discourage non-tolerance of individuals seeking professional assistance. There is no other area of need more so than mental illness where the scriptures challenge our reluctance to gain wisdom. As the world around us change the traditionalism of dogma/doctrine causes the church to remain stagnate on issues where the church should be leading, especially in areas where hope, compassion and support are key. Holding a personal belief that the church of God is a hospital where we all come to see the Great Physician, stigmatizing one illness over another minimizes the miraculous power of God.

Change is inherently difficult, without an understanding. This manuscript will attempt to educate and reveal the plethora of data and resources available to offer guidance and support to families that are suffering in silence. Within the pages are a concert of clinical approaches, medical approaches and biblical approaches to the issues surrounding mental health. All of these approaches are viable paths down a journey of recovery and ultimately supernatural healing to the physiological dysfunctions that warrants a mental health disorder.

Demonization of Mental Illness

Chapter 1

Religious Community Perception of Mental Illness

Dogma/Doctrines

Perception, by definition assumes that there is an understanding of the subject matter. When looking at the understanding of the religious community, there has to be an inclusion of doctrine. Because there are various doctrines driving institutionalized religion in the 21st century. Before making the case for a change in perception, an examination of the doctrinal influences must be visited. As mentioned, while there are various doctrines that exist in the churches, the basic framework of all religions has a tendency to appear very similar in that most believe in an unseen higher power. The need to incorporate religion in the life of an individual has been said to be a psychological necessity. This inherent need for religion has matriculated into what one researcher calls dogmas and superstitions. (1) It is not uncommon for religions to change their doctrine over time, but oddly enough many religions have remained archaic in regard to mental illness. This singular point is critical as these doctrines provide guidelines for which the individual can devise his/her plan for care. While the popular notion is that believers can handle stress and the cares of life more easily, rituals and archaic belief systems can lead to mental ill-heath. Regardless to the various nuances of different religions, the desire for the mental health professionals is to marry the belief system's perception of healing with the proper treatment of the diagnosed illness. Likewise, there is a necessity that mental health professionals incorporate their understanding of the belief system of the patient into the treatment.

For the interest of this writing it is necessary to make the distinction between religion and spirituality. Although people have used these terms interchangeably, there are fundamental differences. The definition we will use for religion and spirituality are the ones introduced in the Journal of Psychiatry:

> *Religion is an organized system of beliefs, practices, rituals, and symbols designed to facilitate closeness to the sacred or transcendent (God, higher power, or ultimate truth/reality). Spirituality is the personal quest for understanding answers to the ultimate questions about life, about meaning, and about relationship with the sacred or transcendent, which may (or may not) lead to or arise from the development of religious rituals and the formation of a community?*

By definition, spirituality would indicate a more inclusive experience, because religion often include socially based ideals and traditions associated with ritualistic and ceremonial activities, but spirituality includes the feelings of the individual in relationship to the overall connection to what he/she believes in. This deep connection drives the sense of value in a person and can have a positive or negative effect on a person suffering with mental illness.

Religion and psychiatry have traditionally been a source of conflict because of the possibility of violating the religious laws established by the doctrinal statements of the religious organization. This conflict when dealing with treatment can cause tremendous anxiety for the patient. Many believe that religion or religious organizations have a responsibility to assess the current state of mental research and the technology that surrounds it to ensure that religion is providing the relief and the possibility of recovery to hurting mankind. However, the need for mental health professionals to incorporate religion into treatment of their patients remains to be a significant hurdle. Noted in many studies is the fact that often psychiatrists and psychologists are statistically less religious than the general population and are in need of additional training which would incorporate religious inquires in the treatment of their patients. It is suggested this would add a level of empathy from the psychiatrists/psychologists for the behavior that is attributed to the religious beliefs. When the only exposure to a particular religious belief is being revealed from the patient's perspective, the treatment is subjected to that point of view, whether negative or positive. Not always will the experience of the patient be a healthy religious outlook, but one that is furthering the depression and anxiety.

In the last several decades scientific research has been done and presented to the public in medical and psychological journals. This material has helped in religious organizations revisiting traditional doctrines that exclude involvement with the mental health community. This course of action has become favorable and has fostered the trend of mental health professionals seeking an understanding of how religious involvement in mature adults affects both medical and mental well-being. The outcome to this trending is a more compassionate approach to the care plan of the individual.

Often the disparity in dogma among religious organizations can dictate access to care or overall denial of a given diagnose. For instance, one study pointed out the huge disparity in United Methodist and Pentecostal clergy in full-time ministry. [2] It was revealed the UM clergy operated out of an informed scientific based understanding, while Pentecostals removed any association to clinical factors and cited the faith of the patient and increased spirituality could combat the diagnosis. In a similar study, 293 Christians approached their leaders in need of help with a personal or family member's mental health illness and found 32% of the time, their leader expressed disagreement that a mental illness diagnosis was correct. Rather cited that the issue was solely one of a spiritual nature and should be addressed with an increase in spiritual exercise. The residue from these responses resulted in almost 15% of these individuals reporting that their faith was negatively impacted and another 12.6% departed their journey of faith all together.

Unfortunately, there is plenty of documentation that outlines the negative experiences individuals suffering with mental illness receive from church leaders and/or the religious community. Often the rhetoric of acceptance is conveyed, but individuals suffering have reported that acceptance was not given. In a study released by Lifeway Research, an evangelical research organization, they stated although many seek help from their church community, they most likely will not receive help on Sunday mornings. The study revealed that most

Protestant senior pastors (66 percent) seldom speak to their congregation about mental illness. (3)

Many believe that this absence in the pulpits of America promote fear and expose ignorance of mental health issues. Although the desire is to move individuals with a disorder to recovery, the church as whole should be prepared to address individuals with a chronic disorder as well as those we consider to be a milder form. To assist congregations in ways to address myths and offer help within the church community Relevant Magazine published these 4 misconceptions and helpful responses. (4) The origin of these misconceptions is born out of the personal experience of Andrea Jongbloed, a Concurrent Disorders Peer Support Coordinator in Canada.

1. People with Mental Health Conditions Are Unsafe.

Most people with mental illnesses are peaceful and respectful of other people. According to the Institute of Medicine, *"Although studies suggest a link between mental illnesses and violence, the contribution of people with mental illnesses to overall rates of violence is small, and further, the magnitude of the relationship is greatly exaggerated in the minds of the general population."*

When the news reports a mentally ill person being violent, consider how it would feel if you had a mental illness rather than subscribing to a culture of fear.

2. People with Mental Illnesses Are Unpredictable and Difficult to Relate to.

I know many people who have professional jobs, raise stable families and also live with a mental illness. When someone is unwell, they may become unpredictable. This is not their normal way of interacting, and many people with mental illnesses have a plan in case they become unwell—for example, informing a family member and adjusting their medications.

Give someone the benefit of the doubt, assume they will be dependable, show up to meetings and relate well. Extend grace and understanding when they are struggling with their mental health. Some people with mental illnesses may have trouble relating to others. Embrace the challenge of interacting with a human being who may have had more struggles in life than you.

3. Most People with Mental Illnesses are on Welfare or Homeless.

Most people with mental illnesses are not homeless. However, as this article from the Washington Post points out, "because the relatively small number of people living on the streets who suffer from paranoia, delusions and other mental disorders are very visible, they have come to stand for the entire homeless population, despite the fact that they are in the minority."

4. People with Mental Illnesses Would Rather Not Talk About it.

It is surprising how open people can be about their mental health journey. One woman I met in church told me she had a mental illness and shared her experience of discrimination because of it.

This conversation depends on the person; some people are very open, and others are private. You may find you are blessed with more awareness when you listen to the struggles of someone with a mental illness. Respect where the person is at with their ability to share, and be open to hearing their mental health struggles.

Real Life Issue

Rick Warren, the famous author of "Purpose Driven Life" and pastor of a mega-church, unfortunately felt the pain of mental illness, after losing his son Matthew to suicide. After this single event many Pastors were forced to address the "elephant in the room"- mental illness in the church. The reluctance to talk openly continues in the 21st century and claim lives that could otherwise be saved. The lack of understanding is the most common reason we flee from the real issue. If the church is made up of the entire population in the community, and 1 in 4 individuals in a year will be affected by mental illness, many of those same individuals occupy the pews. The reality is that the issue of mental illness is not going away and placing them on the prayer list is only part of the solution. A study from Baylor University pointed out that the second most priority of parishioners with family members with mental illness is help from the church. This continues to be a need in our congregations. These same families understand that the love of God extends, even to those we don't understand.

Another area of concern around the issue of mental illness is the question of medicine to treat a disorder. While the majority of the proponents for medication understand the need to assess each individual, it remains a fact that there are many mental health conditions that are physiological. The majority of the mental health professionals agree counseling should be included in treatment, but disregarding medication reflects ignorance of the disorder. A balanced plan of treatment is imperative to ensure recovery. Medication in some case will stabilize chemical imbalances. One professional simply stated in regard to prescribing medication, "Christians get cancer, and they deal with mental illness". Hiding these issues in the dark is often an act of shame. While it is wise to protect the privacy of our loved ones, but a healthy congregation could offer help that can go a long way. Holding to the fact that the church is the Body of Christ, going into the darkest places and facing tough situations demonstrates the light of the God.

A New Approach to Mental Illness in the Church

Throughout this book the deficiencies of the churches response to mental illness will be explored. While it was necessary to highlight the current condition, it is equally necessary to begin to look at a healthier approach. The goal is to make sure the idea of hope is conveyed to every individual that desires to enter into relationship with God. These unknowledgeable individuals come to the church in expectancy that there is an answer for their pain. While we debate on the realities mental health disorders, precious souls continue to sink into holes of despair. This stagnate situation can be energized with an approach to tackle the cancerous perceptions associate to mental illness. The work of removing the notion that every individual experiencing a mental disorder must have a spiritual deficiency has arrived.

One study reveals 68% of all Pastors surveyed thought that there existed in most churches a list of local mental health resources, but only 28% of the members with a family member diagnosed with a mental illness felt there were resources available in their church. The gap between the Pastor's perception and the perception of the families is too large of a gap to foster change, but there are several steps that can be taken to begin to tackle this very large fish. No longer can it remain the responsibility of the Pastor alone. The development of support systems whose work is centered on the mentally ill and their families has been reported as healthy. Often the leader of the organization has an elevated perception, but this can go uncommunicated because of the nature of the topic. If the congregants are not aware of the perception and/or efforts, the problem remains unsolved.

Providing resources and support is huge in developing new strategies for the church. The partnership with the religious community and the mental health community fosters the correct perception. It is a futile effort if two-thirds of the leaders in the church report that they maintain information to connect individuals to local resources, if only a quarter of those needing the information is unaware. In addition to providing education and information, families who attend these churches, desire an open and consistent conversation to help remove the devastating stigma associated with certain illnesses. This stigmatization perpetrates devastating outcomes.

Another new approach suggests motivating Christians as a whole to participate and become educated in the areas of prevention and intervention. Another survey performed by a Christian organization reveal that the communities at large suggest the church isolate efforts toward things like prevention and should be more involved.

Changing Christian College Student's Thoughts

With suicide numbers being extremely large

among college age students, it makes sense to include a new approach for this population of Christians. Researchers have found a single positive article can change the perception of a group of individuals. In addition, it has been reported, the more information an individual has about mental illness the more likely the situation will be treated with compassion and the individual with empathy. This kind of empathetic approach could increase self-esteem of one suffering with a mental disorder. Some professionals have gone as far as to suggest that a single encounter could be the catalyst for recovery.

[1]1. Indian J Psychiatry. 2013 Jan; 55(Suppl 2): S187–S194. doi: 10.4103/0019-5545.105526 PMCID: PMC3705681 Retrieved April 15, 2016, from http://www.ncbi.nlm.nih.gov/pmc/articles/PMC3705681/

2. Copyright © Baylor® University. Retrieved April 15, 2016 from http://www.baylorisr.org/wp-content/uploads/stanford_perceptions.pdf

3. Copyright © 2016 The Christian Post , INC., Retrieved April 15, 2016 from http://www.christianpost.com/news/stigma-of-mental-illness-still-real-inside-the-church-lifeway-research-reveals-126832/

4. Copyright © 2002 Relevant, "4 Misconceptions About Mental Illness and Faith", Retrieved April 15, 2016 from http://www.relevantmagazine.com/god/church/4-misconceptions-about-mental-illness-and-faith

5. Copyright © 2016 • LifeWay Research, Retrieved April 15, 2016 from http://lifewayresearch.com/wp-content/uploads/2014/09/Acute-Mental-Illness-and-Christian-Faith-Research-Report-1.pdf

Chapter 2

Biblical Look at Infirmities

Illness vs Infirmity

Placement of a chapter on infirmities in the middle of this writing warrants an explanation. The case of the physiological existence of symptoms of mental illness is systematically being made. The need to understand infirmities from the biblical perspective is critical in the foundation of the case. Removing the existence of infirmities, also removes the association of mental illness to the disease ideology, thus eliminating a need or hope for healing.

The decision to choose the word infirmities was purposeful to make the point of this chapter. While in many cases illness and infirmity is used interchangeably, infirmity from the perspective of the bible carries a more inclusive meaning. Webster's online dictionary list the meaning of **illness** as a specific condition that prevents your body or mind from working normally: a sickness or disease. Conversely the same website list **infirmity** as a disease or illness that usually lasts for a long time. For the sake of this writing we will utilize this definition as our guide, as this definition is inclusive of illness, thus covering a broad array of diseases. In addition to the definition, this writing will make the argument, in reference to mental illness, that the symptoms of mental illness could be categorized as a diagnosable disease. The medical community has deemed these symptoms are physiological and can be listed with an associated diagnostic code in a published medical manual known as the Diagnostic and Statistical Manual of Mental Disorders (DSM). With this foundation, the biblical examination of infirmities is the next logical step to making the case to work toward mental wholeness in the church.

For the sake of this writing, the King James Version of the bible will be utilized for all scriptural text references as well as any tools for exegesis. Strong's accordance lists the first mention of the word infirmity in Hebrew as *davah* and is found in **Leviticus 12:2**. The Hebrew meaning is to be ill, be unwell. Infirmity, in Greek is *astheneia* and is first found in **Luke 13:11** and is interpreted feebleness (of mind or body). The English word *asthenia* has for its root the same Greek word and according to Webster means lack or loss of strength. These are key to how the Bible project the idea of infirmity/illness. There is a pattern in scripture that reverts to first mentioned and expands on the biblical perspective throughout the Bible. As we build the case for mental wholeness, this is the foundation from which the building begins.

Proper study of the Bible should include contextual reference. Extracting a single verse can often lead to misinterpretation of the thought being conveyed. In the Old Testament scripture cited earlier in Leviticus 12:2, looking at verses 1 through 7 gives a complete thought surrounding the text. The infirmity mentioned here is associated to a woman's condition after she has given birth to a child. Two points are critical here; she is considered ill and anyone that approaches her would also be considered ill. This Old Testament teaching perpetuated the idea that the natural process of a woman's childbirth experience is similar to an illness. There are countless speculations as to why she was considered unclean, but for this writing, investigating those possibilities are beyond the scope. Many believe that the uncleanliness of a Mother after seven days for a boy and 14 days for a girl, although a *sin offering* was required, was not eluding to sin. This may be the case, from a biblical historical perspective, but overall speculations cannot be made. Then the text in Luke 13:11 is housed within the contextual reference of Luke chapter 13 verses 6 through 11. The infirmity mentioned here is clearly a physical one and has caused significant grief for a long period of time. Unlike the previous text there is clearly a compassion that is exuded for this woman because of her illness. Given they are both what the Bible says are infirmities the response to each is totally different. The first inclination is to try and understand the difference between the two, which is simply time.

An attempt to totally understand the minute specifics of the time is not necessary for this writing. While the teachings of the time may not be understood, what is understood today is that society has evolved from at least the behavior associated with the Leviticus text. The majority of people in the 21st century would think it absurd to shun a mother for a week after her giving birth. Removing the tradition of this behavior has provided for numerous positives in assisting a woman during a time that her physical, mental and emotional faculties are experiencing noticeable change. These two examples of how change can be positively affective, there are countless of other examples that reflect progression of mindsets and behaviors evolving as a result of progression in society. Oddly, from statistical analysis, it is reported that mental illness has not experienced the same luxury of progressive thinking. Perhaps the ability to categorize mental health disorders in the disease category is what hinders the progression. Moving society to a new paradigm requires extensive education for the religious community. Often this is a difficult task as the perception is that the progression is in violation of doctrine, dogma or ritualistic customs of the organization.

Where Did It Begin

Embedded in the core of the beliefs of the majority of people in the evangelical religious community, is that because of the actions of Adam in the Garden in the beginning sin entered the earth.

Jesus then is the answer to removing the inherited "condition" from all mankind. It is interesting that the sin stain represented by the disobedient act of Adam is often referred to as the condition of mankind. There is some alignment with this thinking to illness. The question for the Doctor from a Patient is, "what is my condition"? See the correlation? Sin=Condition=Illness=Infirmity. This all in one mentality starts in the foundational teaching of religious doctrines and can be perpetuated negatively in the perspective of an individual, if the distinctions are not clarified.

Let's deal first with sin. Sin's definition from the Bible or from secular study materials have very similar meanings, but for this writing *an immoral act considered to be a transgression against divine law* will be used. The immoral act that was performed by Adam in his disobedience to God was inherited by mankind and thus every man is **born in sin** or some say **born with sin**. Note the difference in terminology can denote two different meanings, but the remedy for both is the same. The position articulated most is the joy of having the "sin" removed when Jesus dies on the cross. However, the residual

25

effect of the disobedience changed the "condition" of the earth. Old Testament biblical teaching says the earth in which Adam dwelled was ALL good: minus anything non-positive. It is then further taught that the change in everything living, altered the genetic makeup of the flesh, thus introducing fragility and vulnerabilities. Given this teaching, there is much conversation around, who and how does one make the distinction of what "parts" of the flesh take on these vulnerabilities. In regard to mental health, too often this thought is lost.

Mental Disorder as Mental Illness

Diagnosable mental disorders are what many call "invisible illnesses" and are often handled poorly by the individual and sometimes those that would offer care and intervention. This kind of behavior stems from stigmas around mental illness in the religious community. When asked if an individual believed they would be welcomed in a church if they were diagnosed with a mental health issue, there exists an alarming contradiction of what between those people who never attend and those who attend church at least once a week. Sadly, those who attend church reveal a 34-point difference in believing they would be welcomed.

These numbers are taken from research done by about 3 years ago and unfortunately, there has not been much change since this time. Much of this kind of response stems from the inability to categorize mental health properly. An effort to move the church forward will require an intentional effort to transform the minds that have housed an incorrect premise for years.

The human tendency is to reject or neglect those things we do not understand. Mental health more so allows this behavior given the disorder is seldom obvious, in reference to any physical distortions. Some could rationalize the fact that it is invisible to give ground to its non-existence. The pain of an individual suffering in silent, undergoing the cruelty of stigmatization and living in the fear of being questioned about their faith walk within the church, is often overwhelming. This type of experience only perpetuates the disorder. Some mature individuals have found coping skills to compensate for the "abnormalities" they experience every day. The concern is for those who feel all alone and the only help they can muster from the community that should be providing support is, chose to be happy. Many feel this is an indictment on the Body, a representation of Jesus Christ. The compassion and concern that drove Him to "die" for sin/illnesses is not being exhibited. Often all that is needed is recognition of the issue and an act of service. This can include simply talking about mental health, handing out resources, being watchful over those with diagnosis and then offering prayer in concert with all the other things the church can do to be of assistance. While mental illness may not be the illness everyone suffers through, the saying says EVERYBODY NEEDS SOMEBODY.

Treading Over Tradition

Every family takes pride in their traditions that are passed on from generation to generation. Many of these traditions are necessary to foster bonds and historical value within the family. As these traditions solidify relationships and build lasting memories, there are also those that lose relevance and can have a negative impact. The church has to be careful not to allow traditions to hinder progressive thinking that will help those hurting in the community. When the traditions take precedence over the individuals that need help, then we have placed more value on the demonstration while lessening the souls of those God has led to us. Culture is always changing and it's a poor body of believers that are not willing to meet the challenges of change.

Jaroslav Jan Pelikan, who authored more than 30 books, was a Sterling Professor of History Emeritus at Yale University and one of the world's foremost scholars of the history of Christianity was quoted as saying:

> *"Tradition is the living faith of the dead, traditionalism is the dead faith of the living. And, I suppose I should add, it is traditionalism that gives tradition such a bad name."*

Many churches in the evangelical community are completely controlled and structured based on the opinions, decisions and mandates of the Founder/Pastor and a small board of that particular congregation. Then there are others that rely on a larger body of representatives that usually consist of the Leaders of several churches who are members of the overall organization. Often traditions cannot be broken because of the tenured individuals that make up the decision making arm of the church or organization. When looking to make the church relevant to today's society, an examination of how the board is established and how decisions are reviewed and decided upon warrants special attention. This does not suggest moving individuals or disbanding boards, but creative ways of inserting ideas and individuals or both can be a great place to begin.

For many congregations that make up the religious community, change is often frightening. Change for some is threatening as it will challenge the ideology of those that follow. The possibility of losing "individuals" that have been long time participants and contributors is a familiar consideration within the circle of leaders of churches/organizations. The Reverend James Martin, a Jesuit priest writes in a Cable News Network (CNN) blog that in a recent meeting of the Catholic Synod, no changes were made to the doctrine, in fact any suggestion of change was met with outrage. [2] One of the most amazing things he wrote in the article was the obstinacy to change was strong and even the Pope would have difficulty making changes. Perhaps this really is a question of why is change so adamantly resisted in the religious community? Reverend Martin believes that the

Catholic Church for instance has merged the idea of dogma and doctrine, explaining dogma as the foundational principles of the organization and doctrine as the outlining of how to exercise those principles listed in the dogma. This line of thinking is dangerous, because legitimately if they are as intertwined as believed, then touching one touches the other.

With the aforementioned premise in the Catholic church mentioned previously, there is a similar thought process emanating out of the evangelical church. This non-productive progress reeks of legalism and places the church in a dilapidated state. The freedom written in the Bible in what is known as the Gospels, is completely contradicted by this failed reasoning. What is found over and over in these profound books of the Bible is Jesus changing or treading over laws and traditions that hindered a loving, compassionate and empathetic response to an individual. Today's church must emulate this same behavior else it tramples over the sanctity of the example of Jesus.

The encouragement to understand illness from a biblical perspective, re-examine traditions and prepare for change is being motivated by the changing of the demographics in congregations across the country. The demographic of young people in our society growing the quickest are those who the researchers call Millennials.

These are individuals born after 1980 and are labeled Millennials because they all come of age after the turn of the Millennium (2000). This group of young people continue to be a target population for advertisement and marketing campaigns because of the large number that make up the population in the U.S. When focused on this group, it was revealed that their belief in God is the lowest among these individuals, but their concern for community and acceptance of mental illness is more than 50% higher than other demographic groups. Pew Research goes on to reveal that other religious practices remained comparable to the other demographic groups. In addition, daily prayer remained a continued focus for Millennials. Three areas where older adults were similar were:

- Belief in the After Life
- Belief in the Existence of Heaven and Hell
- Belief in Miracles

A survey of 900 young people by a group of University students revealed 85 percent said they were comfortable with individuals diagnosed with a mental disorder. With this new found elevation of thinking, comes the acceptance of mental health diagnosis and/or mental health treatment. The enormous benefit of having these individuals in congregations all over the country, is a measureable leap in removing stigma of mental illness. The idea that illness is illness is illness is gaining momentum in our society as a whole. If the church is posed to be reflective of our society, demographically and the reflection of the compassion of Jesus simultaneously, there has to be a push toward this goal.

Finally, it is also necessary to point out the fact that more individuals' ion Generation Y(Millennials) are being diagnosed with mental illnesses. At first glance professionals believed this was because of the evolution of acceptance in society, but a closer look revealed another possibility. This generation of young people are known for their attitude of entitlement and are frequently are stressed about issues that older generations simply accepted. In addition to individual attitudes, some believe that something called "helicopter parenting" have hindered these young people coming to a place of independence because of the constant hovering of the parents. This poses a unique situation in that statistics are encouraging in this situation as those millennials that are accepting to mental illness will have the opportunity to extend compassion, empathy and hope to those suffering with a mental health disorder. As stated by Betty Brian of *Brain World*, [3] "– mental illness is a very real issue faced by younger people, and because of this, the need for improved healthcare resources is more pressing than ever."

1

[1]1. Copyright © 2016 Christianity Today, "Mental Illness and the Church: New Research on Mental Health from LifeWay Research",Ed Stetzer, September 2013, Retrieved April 18, 2016 from http://www.christianitytoday.com/edstetzer/2013/september/mental-illness-and-church-new-research-on-mental-health-fro.html

2. Copyright © 2016 Cable News Network. Turner Broadcasting System, Inc., "Why are some Catholics so afraid of change?", The Rev. James Martin, October 2015 Retrieved April 18, 2016 from http://www.cnn.com/2015/10/26/world/catholics-fear-change/index.html

3. Copyright © 2015 BRAIN WORLD, "Millennial Mental Health", October 2015, Retrieved April 18, 2016 from http://brainworldmagazine.com/millennial-mental-health/

Chapter 3

Demonization of Mental Illness

Moving the Mark

In the previous chapter the origin of illness from a biblical perspective was discussed. This chapter will build on this premise and explore the spiritualization of certain illnesses. Medical issues for the most part have been openly accepted as physiological altering and deemed the object for prayer. Mental health issues on the other hand have not been so readily categorized, thus leaving these issues either unaddressed or improperly addressed by the evangelical religious community. This chapter will explore some of the myths and erroneous information that supports this unproductive behavior. The criticality of moving the mindsets of the church is paramount in this book. The absence of understanding most often leads to improper handling of a situation. The issue of mental wholeness in the church is much too important to transforming and building strong followers to simply remain in the traditions of the thinking of times past. Adjusting the mindset regarding an issue does not always require the dismantling of traditions and/or dogma, but it does require a shift in positioning. This positioning offers new hope to those experiencing a mental disorder AND operating in the church.

Mental Health History

From a historical perspective, many cultures explained mental illness as demonic possession. These negative attitudes perpetuated an atmosphere of stigma of in the United States around the 18th century. [1] This degrading perception fueled the way for confinement of mentally ill individuals. Dorothea Dix, an activist in the 1840's worked to move these individuals from the poor living conditions she had witnessed to psychiatric hospitals. This did not occur overnight, but it took her 40-years to persuade the U.S. government to fund the building of these institutions. Eventually 32 state run psychiatric hospitals were erected. There were several reasons why institutionalization was welcomed. The biggest reason was that before these institutions, families and communities were having difficulties caring for their relatives. This worked fine for a period of time, but soon the conditions of these facilities decayed, because of the lack of funding and the lack of professionals to staff the institutions.

By the mid-1950s the development of new drugs facilitated the deinstitutionalization of these facilities. Antipsychotic drugs allowed many patients to utilize outpatient treatment. Many believed this treatment was more productive as community-oriented care added an additional level of support which afforded patients a higher quality of life. In 1963 the Community Health Centers Act pushed for standards that would only institutionalize those "who posed an imminent danger to themselves or someone else". This change was seen in a dramatic decrease in institutionalized patients between 1950 and 1980, from 560,000 to 130,000.

Although deinstitutionalization was driven by a single goal – improving care and quality of life – the efforts became a source of focus for researchers and resulted in high polarization. Soon studies surfaced that revealed the lack of treatment for other aspects of health care failing resources among mentally ill patients in the communities. In addition, instances of poverty, inadequate living conditions, and loneliness were reported. Those that opposed deinstitutionalization argued that it had simply become "trans institutionalization", where the community based psychiatric care centers and the criminal justice system were interdependent. The burden of care for these unfortunate individuals had simply fallen on the prison system. They went on to point out that the severely mentally ill patients were a minority and warranted a closer look at the data collected from this "clinically and demographically distinct population". Today there are continued efforts in the United States to improve services and treatment in community based programs and facilities.

Criminalization of the Mentally Ill

As stated above, the failure of the community-based psychiatric care has been blamed for the increase in the incarceration of individuals with mental illness. The National Alliance for the Mentally Ill (NAMI) estimates twenty to forty percent of the mentally ill in America come in contact with the criminal justice system. Many of the jails/prisons are ill equipped to deal with these special needs inmates and often they are left to confinement or the challenge to coexist with a prison population that further exploits their vulnerability.

The Huffington Post's Ginger Lerner-Wren asked the question on the Healthy Living blog page, Have We Reached a Flashpoint in regard to the criminalization of the mentally ill in America, [2] She reported that the Human Rights Watch published a 223-page report entitled ***Ill-Equipped*** which outlined the gross treatment of inmates of some of the country's largest prisons. With more than 10 times the number of mentally ill patients in treatment facilities currently residing in the prison system, there is a call for reform.

One forensic psychiatrist went as far as to say, "the criminalization of the mentally ill is nothing short of a national tragedy". [3] The need to collaborate with leaders of law enforcement and government is urgent. With approximately 2 million people suffering with severe mental illness, the focus is on outcomes that will prioritize treatment and recovery, which will help in lowering recidivism rates. Reform has to consider alternatives to incarceration, that include policy makers in collaboration with the courts and community treatment efforts. This ensures mutual ownership once the policy is implemented. Although there is little research available, the estimation of the impact of mentally ill individuals entering the criminal justice system is alarming. Below are some observations about the burden of criminal costs in California for the mentally ill.

- Total impact of the mentally ill on the criminal justice and corrections system: adding up all the low estimates would result in an overall cost of about $1.2 billion, while adding up the high estimates would give an overall total of about $1.8 billion.
- Research has shown that 8 to 20 percent of state prison inmates are seriously mentally ill. Adding up the prison and parole costs under an 8 percent scenario would result in a total state corrections cost of $245 million for handling the seriously mentally ill in 1995-96.

Under the 20-percent scenario, the total cost would be $619 million.

- The percentage of county jail inmates who are seriously mentally ill has been estimated to be between 7.2 and 15 percent. The jail and probation costs under the 7.2 percent scenario would be $58.4 million. Under the 15 percent scenario, the cost would be $118 million.

- It is conservatively estimated that 10 percent of all arrestees are seriously mentally ill. This would imply that city police departments in California spent $445 million on handling mentally ill offenders. For county sheriffs, the total would be $160 million.

- The corrections and criminal justice costs associated with seriously mentally ill offenders may represent a possible misallocation of scarce space and resources. If some of these offenders could be dealt with in some alternative way, e.g. certain more cost-effective treatment programs, it could make room in correctional facilities for other convicted criminals who are not being incarcerated because of lack of space.

- The existing empirical data is very mixed regarding alternative treatment programs such as outpatient programs. Some studies show the potential and promise of such programs while others offer pessimistic numbers on important factors such as recidivism rates.

These estimations are comparative across the country, but Renee Binder of the American Psychiatric Association (APA) suggest that there is some progress being made as suggested in the list of several bills that address the issue of incarcerated mentally ill patients. Those bills include the Comprehensive Justice and Mental Health Act, the Comprehensive Addiction and Recovery Act of 2015, the Helping Families in Mental Health Crisis Act of 2015, and the Mental Health Reform Act of 2015. Through these efforts of our local government and law enforcement the goal to treat and not punish can be recognized.

From Criminalization to Demonization

The idea of mentally ill individuals trying to navigate the justice system has proven to be unsuccessful. Therefore, our prison systems remain full with the burden of criminally rehabbing the mentally ill. The treatment plans for criminals are vastly different than for the mentally ill. The probability of this individual leaving the prison different or even better than when he entered is statistically impossible if specific treatment has not been provided. The push to understand and track these instances, gives way to community based models that will be developed to provide specialized care and support. These communities based models also open opportunities for religious organizations to get involved. Like most programs and initiatives there are model structures that have to be addressed and developed. A model which would include the church as a community resource represents positive advancement toward holistic treatment of the mentally ill.

Exploring the model that include the religious community calls for education and training on the topic of mental illness to assist in moving the mindset of the church beyond the demonization of mental illness. The travesty would be in the double victimization of these individuals. As discussed in earlier chapters, there remains a level of stigmatization in the church that presents huge apprehension from many professionals.

With only four-percent of Pastors mentioning mental illness only on a monthly basis, the need for Pastors and congregants to engage in education is apparent. Knowing when to refer serious cases of mental health disorders is at the top of the list of educational concerns for leaders. The follow-up to training for leaders, is for church members to gain information, education and training which would lift the levels of empathy for those suffering.

Educating the Church

Moving individuals from the traditional thinking surrounding mental illness, will require education on the basics of biological brain malfunctions. Too often people are guided by the traditional teaching of the church, where strange behavior, primarily by those experiencing a psychotic break, is demon possession at best or demonically induced. Not excusing the possibility that there are those in the church who are demon possessed as it is a real phenomenon, but these are not the same. This kind of thinking perpetuate the isolation, rejection and stigmatization mentally unhealthy individuals experience. Given some time in scripture and in educational material would assist the church in moving forward and formulating ministry for the mentally unhealthy.

Because the church has operated so long in traditionalism as it pertains to the archaic teaching around mental health. The mention of mentally illness and demon possession is recorded in the Bible and there is a distinction between the two. (5) For instance, in the New Testament Mark 5:1-16 and Luke 8:26-37, Jesus encounters a man the Bible clearly identifies as one that was possessed.

> **Mark 5:1** *And they came over unto the other side of the sea, into the country of the Gadarenes.* **2** *And when he was come out of the ship, immediately there met him out of the tombs a man with an unclean spirit,* **3** *Who had his dwelling among the tombs; and no man could bind him, no, not with chains:* **4** *Because that he had been often bound with fetters and chains, and the chains had been plucked asunder by him, and the fetters broken in pieces: neither could any man tame him.* **5** *And always, night and day, he*

was in the mountains, and in the tombs, crying, and cutting himself with stones. **6** But when he saw Jesus afar off, he ran and worshipped him, **7** **And cried with a loud voice, and said, What have I to do with thee, Jesus, thou Son of the most high God? I adjure thee by God, that thou torment me not.** **8** For he said unto him, Come out of the man, thou unclean spirit. **9** And he asked him, What is thy name? And he answered, saying, My name is Legion: for we are many. **10** And he besought him much that he would not send them away out of the country. **11** Now there was there nigh unto the mountains a great herd of swine feeding. **12** And all the devils besought him, saying, Send us into the swine, that we may enter into them. **13** And forthwith Jesus gave them leave. And the unclean spirits went out, and entered into the swine: and the herd ran violently down a steep place into the sea, (they were about two thousand;) and were choked in the sea. **14** And they that fed the swine fled, and told it in the city, and in the country. And they went out to see what it was that was done. **15**

And they come to Jesus, and see him that was possessed with the devil, and had the legion, sitting, and clothed, and in his right mind : and they were afraid. **16** *And they that saw it told them how it befell to him that was* **possessed with the devil,** *and also concerning the swine.*

There are several similarities in the actions of this man as in one that is mentally unstable, but in addition to those areas he displayed supernatural spiritual power. For instance:

- The demons had supernatural power to break the chains
- The demons knew who Jesus was before He approached him
- The demons knew that Jesus was the Messiah
- The demons were causing the man to speak.

This wasn't the first time Jesus encountered a demon. In Mark 1:32-34 and Luke 4:33-36. So clearly there is record of demon possession, but there is also record of mental illness. If scripture will take care in the making the distinction, the ability to understand the difference is revealed in the Word for all to know. In Deuteronomy 28:27-29, 1 Samuel 21:12-15, Mark 3:20-21 and Acts 26:24-25. The record in Deuteronomy interprets the Hebrew word for insane as madness in verse number 28. See the scripture below in context:

> **Deuteronomy 28:22** *The LORD shall smite thee with a consumption, and with a fever, and with an inflammation, and with an extreme burning, and with the sword, and with blasting, and with mildew; and they shall pursue thee until thou perish.* **23** *And thy heaven that is over thy head shall be brass, and the earth that is under thee shall be iron.* **24** *The LORD shall make the rain of thy land powder and dust: from heaven shall it come down upon thee, until thou be destroyed.* **25** *The LORD shall cause thee to be smitten before thine enemies: thou shalt go out one way against them, and flee seven ways before them: and shalt be removed into all the kingdoms of the earth.* **26** *And thy carcase shall be meat unto all fowls of the air, and unto the beasts of the earth, and no man shall fray them away.* **27** *The LORD will smite thee with the botch of Egypt, and with the*

emerods , and with the scab, and with the itch, whereof thou canst not be healed . **28 The LORD shall smite thee with madness, and blindness, and astonishment of heart:** *29 And thou shalt grope at noonday, as the blind gropeth in darkness, and thou shalt not prosper in thy ways: and thou shalt be only oppressed and spoiled evermore, and no man shall save thee. 30 Thou shalt betroth a wife, and another man shall lie with her: thou shalt build an house, and thou shalt not dwell therein: thou shalt plant a vineyard, and shalt not gather the grapes thereof. 31 Thine ox shall be slain before thine eyes, and thou shalt not eat thereof: thine ass shall be violently taken away from before thy face, and shall not be restored to thee: thy sheep shall be given unto thine enemies, and thou shalt have none to rescue them. 32 Thy sons and thy daughters shall be given unto another people, and thine eyes shall look, and fail with longing for them all the day long: and there shall be no might in thine hand. 33 The fruit of thy land, and all thy labours, shall a nation which thou knowest* *not eat up; and thou shalt be only oppressed and crushed alway: **34** So that thou shalt be mad for the sight of thine eyes which thou shalt see.*

Author Nick Lane says in his book, *"Depressed or Possessed? Christians Recognizing and Responding to Mental Illness"*, addressing the question of how do we know the difference. [6]

- Take a history. Has there been extensive involvement in witchcraft or the occult?
- Are the symptoms atypical of psychiatric or physical illness? Are there explanations other than demonic possession?
- Is there agreement between level-headed Christians who have spent time praying and seeking the will of God on the matter?
- Remember that Jesus only exorcised when asked to do so or when manifestations occurred in front of him – he did not go to people and tell them that they needed to be exorcised.

Again the Word of God makes a distinction between illness and demon-possession which is illustrated clearly in Matthew 4:24. There were those that were sick, diseased, tormented, possessed, lunatic and palsy brought to Him and the Bible said He healed them all. Not only is there a distinction, the text shares the good news that He also healed them. The hopelessness that mentally ill individuals suffer with can be relieved if the Word could just be shared without judgment.

Finally, demon possession can be categorized as a spiritual problem, but mental illness can be a collaboration of social, spiritual, psychological or physical ailments that hinder an individual from performing in the realm of normalcy he/she is accustomed to. Although there is a certain level of complexity associated with making the distinction, the church must rely on the ability to know spiritual things through what it known as discernment. This is a critical area as without prayerful discernment, it is easy to make the wrong distinction when it comes to mentally ill individuals. The disaster of a mentally unhealthy person coming to the church for help and safety and in turn receives further stigmatization, rejection and hatred, is criminal. The house of /God is a place of refuge in the community. All should be able to come! Categorizing illnesses is dangerous, as limits are now placed on what God can and will heal. If a cancer patient is directed to the care of her oncologist, the heart patient to his cardiologist and arthritis patient to the rheumatologist why not the manically depressed person encouraged to see the psychologist/psychiatrist.

1. Copyright © 2000-2015 Unite For Sight, Inc.
Retrieved April 18 2016, from
http://www.uniteforsight.org/mental-health/module2

2. Copyright © 2016 TheHuffingtonPost.com, Inc.,"The
Criminalization of the Mentally Ill in America — Have We
Reached a Flashpoint?", September 2014,
Retrieved April 18 2016, from
http://www.huffingtonpost.com/ginger-lernerwren/the-
criminalization-of-th_b_5607820.html

3. Copyright © 2016 American Psychiatric Association,
"Working to Decriminalize Mental Illness", Renée Binder M.D.,
Retrieved April 18 2016, from
https://psychiatry.org/news-room/apa-blogs/apa-
blog/2015/10/working-to-decriminalize-mental-illness

4. Copyright © 2016 Mental Health America of
California, "Corrections, Criminal Justice, and the Mentally Ill:
Some Observations About Costs in California",
By Lance T. Izumi, J.D., Mark Schiller, M.D. and
Steven Hayward, Ph.D., September 1996,
Retrieved April 18 2016, from
http://www.mhac.org/pdf/PacificResearchStudy.pdf

5. Copyright Messiah's House of Yahvah, "Demon
Possession vs. Mental Illness", Retrieved April 18 2016, from
http://messiahshouseofyahvah.org/ArticlesAndMore/DemonPosse
ssion.V.MentalIllness.html

6. Copyright © Believer's Brain 2012, "Demons and
Mental Illness", November 2012, Retrieved April 18 2016, from
https://believersbrain.com/2012/11/29/demons-and-mental-
illness/[2]

2

Demonization of Mental Illness

Chapter 4

Spirit, Soul and Body

Human Well-being

This chapter will include several definitions of words as the search to understand wholeness begins. Many are typically very familiar to most, but the purpose of assigning definitions in this writing is to make sure the reader and writer are on the same page. Because of the commonality of some words, we can actually overlook a more appropriate definition for the case. The ultimate goal is make the point that the concern of God is the whole of mankind.

The idea of being whole is not a 21st century idea nor a theological premise ignored by individuals not associated with a religious affiliation. Mankind will always have an innate drive to reach a sense of "completeness" or "wholeness" in their existence. The absence of this satisfaction is what is commonly blamed for the use of outside stimuli to achieve the "sense" of wholeness. Wholeness by definition is recorded in Webster as physically sound and healthy; free of disease or deformity; mentally or emotionally sound. While many argue if this is humanly possible, the chase for it is ever looming.

Balance is key in seeking wholeness explained by an article on the About.com website on their Healthy Living page. (1) It is common to have physical manifestations as a result of a mind that is overloaded and emotions in chaos. Looking into four areas this chapter will discuss the interconnectivity of these parts that make up 4 areas of every human.

- Physical Well-Being
- Emotional Well-Being
- Mental Health and Wellness
- Spirituality

Physical Well-Being

First, the physical body tends to demand the most attention, not only because it is the visible part of man, but also because all of the other areas are manifested or endured through the body. Many believe that caring for the body will take some personal assessment, including learning how to listen to the body as it speaks. The body speaks loudest through pain and immediate attention can help to ward off long-term, chronic illnesses. When the body is not able to function in the "normal" capacity, emotions enter as those things that are enjoyed have been eliminated. This can ultimately affect the mental wellness and usher in a level of depression from the lack of normalcy and enjoyment.

Emotional Well-Being

Secondly, like the previous area, emotional stability helps to balance the body, it is not uncommon for illnesses to surface when the emotional health is compromised. Maintaining a level of wellness in the emotions can be accomplished in many ways, as many ways as is unique to each individual.

Healing emotions are tricky because often the individual has to invest time and effort in learning and attending self-care. Too often emotional distress is driven by painful memories and the desire or resources to tackle these emotions are not there. The danger in this is the refusal to address what is now known to be a bother, suppression only guarantees it will surface again and one can never know what is happening while it is festering within.

Mental Health and Wellness

Thirdly, this area is commonly avoided. There are many reasons suggested, one of the most common answers to the question revolves around stigmatization. Most people want to believe that they are for the most part mentally well. To think otherwise would suggest that one is "crazy". Avoiding the evidence is a common mistake as suppressed mental un-wellness could very well lead to more severe case of the illness and even an introduction to physical ailments. Previous chapters have hinted, addressed and outlined many of the reasons mental wellness should be addressed quickly, therapeutically or medically, whatever the case requires.

Spirituality

Lastly, this area is most commonly ignored, because it is used interchangeably with being religious, which signifies for some people church attendance. Regardless of what many believe for themselves, it is very possible for a person to be spiritual and not be affiliated with a church. Although, this makes it more difficult to assess the wellness of spirituality as there has to be a guide in which to make comparisons to. Assessing wellness here is necessary, but also extremely fragile. For instance, in relationship to mental illness, individuals suffering a severe mental disorder such as schizophrenia, have reported ongoing conversations with demonic forces. This is VERY spiritual, but not healthy for the patient's mental health and certainly not their spiritual health. Although, these four areas are a good starting place to assess wholeness, the quest for wholeness is ongoing and ever evolving.

God's Divine Design

The complexity of man can never be completely understood by the human mind. God offered no blueprint that would allow man to recreate himself with the same accuracy created in the first man, Adam. The nature of mankind is not duplicated in any other creatures of God. All that is known is discovered from study and research. Exact reproduction is impossible and every attempt has fallen short. In this chapter a look at the nature of mankind will serve as foundation for the case of wholeness for God's people.

Faith and Health Connection, a nonprofit Christian health ministry examines Biblical truths and principles, as well as medically-sound guidelines, to assist individuals to obtain wholeness. On this website there are discussions in reference to two schools of thought in regard to the nature of mankind; tripartite(trichotomy) view and bipartite(dichotomy) view. (2) Bipartite suggest that there are two parts of mankind, which are comprised of the body and soul/spirit, but for the sake of this writing the tripartite view serves as a more appropriate perspective. Here the soul and the spirit are looked at distinctly instead of the same entity. In short, man is a spirit with a soul(mind) which lives in a body. The ideal biblical text that this writing will use for the basis for the trichotomy of man is displayed in 1

Thessalonians 5:23. Here the writer conveys the two distinct immaterial parts of the human nature. Below is this scripture within context.

> *1 Thessalonians 5:18 In every thing give thanks : for this is the will of God in Christ Jesus concerning you. 19 Quench not the Spirit. 20 Despise not prophesyings. 21 Prove all things; hold fast that which is good. 22 Abstain from all appearance of evil. 23 And the very God of peace sanctify you wholly; and I pray God your whole **spirit** and **soul** and **body** be preserved blameless unto the coming of our Lord Jesus Christ. 24 Faithful is he that calleth you, who also will do it. 25 Brethren, pray for us. 26 Greet all the brethren with an holy kiss. 27 I charge you by the Lord that this epistle be read unto all the holy brethren. 28 The grace of our Lord Jesus Christ be with you. Amen.*

The first part of the trichotomy referenced in the text is *spirit* or the Greek word *pneuma*, which is translated as spirit in the scriptures 111 times and Holy Ghost more than 85 times. This is the part of mankind that desires to know God and seeks to delight Him. Only this part of the human nature has any knowledge of those things in the spirit or that which is spiritual. Therefore, it is believed that it is this part of the human nature that has to be reborn as it has taken on the nature of sinful flesh at birth. This point is crucial in understanding the soul(mind) because of the interwoven closeness of these two entities it is not unthinkable that one effects the other. The health of the spirit can dictate the health of the soul(mind) or vice-versa.

The second part of the trichotomy referenced in 1 Thessalonians 5:23 is *soul* or the Greek word *psyche*, which is where we get our English words psychology, psychiatrist and psyche. Although this same Greek word is translated with multiple definitions throughout the scriptures, the thought in this text is to introduce the trichotomy of man. Because spirit and soul are often used interchangeably and we find both here, the assumption is that the writer is making a distinction. Some theologians believe that the struggle experienced is the fight for control of the soul by the flesh and the spirit. Assuming the spirit has been transformed to be in relationship with God the conflict with the flesh is immediate as the same transformation has not taken place. The flesh still houses the desires to live destructively and operate with negative persuasion, but the spirit thrives for the complete opposite. The mind now operates as the control center for behavior and can be influenced by the spirit or the flesh. Thus, writers of the New Testament letter often make references to the battle that will continuously exist for mankind in the earth realm. The behavior manifestation is the result of which voice – flesh or spirit – the mind yielded to at the time. This analogy so closely resembles the activity of an individual that suffering with a mental health diagnosis such as schizophrenia. The battle to decide which voice to listen to just became more intense as more voices are introduced. The mind then has a tremendous responsibility of remaining well. Some theologians believe the mind is the center of all things and have isolated 3 key categories that the activity of the mind can be categorized into; (3) volition/will, intellect/reason and emotion/feeling.

The third and final part of the trichotomy referenced is *body* or the Greek word *sōma*, which is translated body over 144 times in the Bible. The more obvious of the three areas of mankind is this area. Clearly this word references the outer part of an individual which houses the other two areas. While often in scripture text this same word is translated sinful nature, this eludes to the theological premise that what is hidden in the flesh is this nature that is contrary to the things of God. The recanting of the creation, introduces the "dirtiness" of flesh in Genesis 2:7. Researchers have found that the same elements that are found in soil are also found in the human body. With this as a backdrop, it is no wonder there's a need for the spirit to be changed in order to combat the mind.

God in His sovereign-ness made man with these three areas and did not leave us without clear instructions on how to operate. As mentioned earlier these 3 areas of mankind have been mentioned throughout scripture, both individually and also together. Romans 7 paints a clear picture of all three working in concert for the good of man.

> ***Romans 7:18*** *For I know that in me (that is, <u>in my flesh(**body**)</u>,) dwelleth no good thing: for to will is present with me; but how to perform that*

*which is good I find not.   **19** For the good that I would I do not: but the evil which I would not, that I do.   **20** Now if I do that I would not, it is no more * I that do it, but sin that dwelleth in me.   **21** I find then a law, that, when I would do good, evil is present with me.   **22** For I delight in the law of God after <u>the inward man(**spirit**)</u>:   **23** But I see another law in my members, warring against the law of <u>my mind(**soul**)</u>, and bringing me into captivity to the law of sin which is in my members.   **24** O wretched man that I am! who shall deliver me from the body of this death?   **25** I thank God through Jesus Christ our Lord. So then with the mind I myself serve * the law of God; but with the flesh the law of sin.*

The words of this scripture text bring the trichotomy into clear focus. What we see here is the ***spirit*** giving divine suggestion, seeking to please God, but the ***body*** is thirsting for the sin nature housed within and the ***soul*** is called upon to make the final decision. Can you imagine the outcome when the mind, the psyche is compromised by a mental health disorder?

State of Being

Too often when asked the question, how are you, many stop at the momentary condition of the body. While this is one way of conveying your wellness, there is a need to teach individuals to assess the whole man: spirit, soul and body. As previously establish, mankind is a trichotomy and all three parts are interwoven so as to have the ability to effect the other part. It is typical to use state-of-being as a question about the physical condition and state-of-mind as a question about the mental condition. State-of-mind is basically specific and direct and eludes to the mental health of an individual. This question includes the inquiry about the emotional, psychological and social well-being. Here there must be a note that the absence of a diagnosable mental health disorder does not indicate good mental health. Because good mental health examines everything from relationships current to relationships past and the emotional status within those relationships about the other person as well as yourself. On the other hand, state-of-being is more indirect. Although it is customary to answer in regard to the physical, the condition of the mind, body or soul could drive the answer. A well body and a broken spirit equals an unhealthy state-of-being. A well body and a troubled mind equals an unhealthy state-of-being. Too often both a broken spirit and a troubled mind have led to an unhealthy body. The divine alignment of all three in their healthy place produces wholeness.

Health and Wellness

The most common used definition for health *is the condition of being well or free from disease*, as stated in Webster's Dictionary. The definition for wellness is *the quality or state of being healthy*. As similar as these two may sound, they are suggesting different state-of-beings. Medical News Today (4) reported definitions for wellness from two different research universities as:

> *"a state of optimal well-being that is oriented toward maximizing an individual's potential. This is a life-long process of moving towards enhancing your physical, intellectual, emotional, social, spiritual, and environmental well-being."* - **Mickinley Health Center, University of Illinois**

"the integration of mind, body and spirit. Optimal wellness allows us to achieve our goals and find meaning and purpose in our lives. Wellness combines seven dimensions of well-being into a quality way of living. Overall, wellness is the ability to live life to the fullest and to maximize personal potential in a variety of ways. Wellness involves continually learning and making changes to enhance your state of wellness. When we balance the physical, intellectual, emotional, social, occupational, spiritual, and environmental aspects of life, we achieve true wellness." - **University of East Carolina**

The two definitions are indicative of the various perspectives available in the area of health and wellness. The common thread between the two is the idea of wellness being a life-long journey. This then would suggest that an individual could be as well they can at a given moment with the resources, environment and community available, but have a change in a particular area that affects their wellness positively or negatively. The overarching goal is to seek to maintain wellness over time, making whatever adjustments are necessary to achieve it. Not seeking the ultimate level could lead to repercussions in the mind, body and soul.

By no means have the topic of wellness been exhausted, but rather the surface has been thoroughly scratched. Condensing this broad topic to a single definition would be dangerous for the readers, thus the abundance of views has been presented. After discussing what wellness is, there must be a statement about what wellness is not. Wellness is not hedonism. Because an individual is well, does not also indicate that everything is pleasurable. In actuality the chase for all things of pleasure could result in an unhealthy state-of-being. To avoid the pitfalls of seeking health and wellness from a personal perspective without guidelines, Medical News Today list on their websites the determinates of health:

- Where we live
- The state of our environment
- Genetics
- Our income
- Our education level

- Our relationship with friends and family.

Examining the list of determinates, half of them are out of our control. Without being in a healthy mental state it would be hard to maintain health and wellness in the economy and atmosphere of the country today. The ability to set and attain goals for the latter half of the list will reveal where we really are on the level wellness. Often the collapse of income, inability to matriculate higher education and poor relationships can catapult an individual into negative mental wellness. It has been discovered an individual's socioeconomic status is often equivalent to their level of health. Conversely, the obvious is true for those on the lower end of the socioeconomic. Lastly, one area that had a huge impact on the health and well-being of an individual is their environment. In light of the water crisis in Flint, it is possible that there are many people who are not well and without physical symptoms, but a darkened sense of doom given the lack of attention and concern exhibited by the local government. The crisis removed a sense of safety and therefore compromised good health.

As this chapter has exposed, there plenty of variables to consider when assessing wholeness, health and wellness. The attempt to move the religious community to a place of awareness in regard to wholeness will most likely take more research and conversation. The wellness topic includes mental health, and not until the bigger piece is openly discussed the more complex issues will never make into the discussion.

3

---

1. Copyright © 2016 About.com, "Mind, Body, Spirit" Retrieved April 20, 2016 from http://healing.about.com/od/healthyliving/u/mindbodyspirit.htm

2. Copyright © 2016 Faith and Health Connection, Retrieved April 20, 2016 from http://www.faithandhealthconnection.org/the_connection/spirit-soul-and-body/

3. Copyright © 2014 Hell Hades and the Afterlife, Retrieved April 20, 2016 from http://www.hellhadesafterlife.com/hell/mind-body-spirit

4. Copyright © 2003 Medical News Today, "Public Health Mental Health What Is Health? What Does Good Health Mean?", by Christian Nordqvist, July 2015 Retrieved April 20, 2016 from http://www.medicalnewstoday.com/articles/150999.php

Chapter 5:

Clinical Recovery and/or Spiritual Healing

Establishing New Hope

This chapter will take a look at healing from a clinical perspective, a spiritual perspective and the all so often overlooked joint healing. While it has been customary to look at these instances as separate, it is important to understand the value of following clinical directives, while praying for a miraculous intervention or spiritual healing. This is not a new concept, but given the traditional approach to mental illness it is one not openly agreed upon in the church. Before examining this approach, a couple points need to be made. First, establishing mental disorders as an illness and secondly the existence of modern day miracles. Together these points will offer new hope for mentally ill patients.

The aforementioned spiritual healing deserves an explanation, in light of the previous chapters that argue the demonization of mental illness. The phraseology here is speaking specifically about the type of healing, not the type of disease. Individuals whom believe in modern day miracles pray daily for miraculous intervention into whatever illness the individual may be suffering. This does not refute the clinical diagnosis of the disease nor the anticipation of a miraculous intervention. Ultimately, a believer would attribute all healing to God, no matter the path to healing they may have chosen. Some argue that submitting to the directives of the Doctor for a particular illness nullifies the element of faith. At the same time others believe that to disregard the directives of a Doctor after a clinical diagnosis is ignorance. For this chapter, the writer advocates submitting to the directives of the Doctor.

Mental health disorders are mainly diagnosed by signs and symptoms. These signs and symptoms are categorized in alignment with diagnosis descriptions listed in the Diagnostic and Statistical Manual of Mental Disorder (DSM), yielding a particular disease diagnosis. Currently, there are no laboratory tests that can be performed to make the diagnosis, but various interview tools and assessments help in making a clinical determination. Medical/Mental history is also considered when observing signs and symptoms. The three areas most evaluated in assessing an individual is work, activities and relationships. For instance, when an individual is expressing an inability to focus at work, diminished interest in activities and a negative change in in relationships for over a two-week period, he/she can be diagnosed as clinically depressed. Early on, this situation does not warrant medical or therapeutic intervention, but an individual who notices these changes should remain alert, regarding the escalation of these symptoms. At the time the individual deems medical intervention is necessary, there are several options for accessing care including the Primary Care Physician. Care in this case could include therapy with a psychologist or therapy and medication which then may include a psychiatrist. The collaboration of these clinicians would at some point evaluate the previous condition of the individual and would pronounce "clinical healing": where the signs and symptoms at the onset have diminished or no longer remain.

The subject of clinical healing for mentally ill individuals is a continuous topic of discussion in the mental health professional community. Clinical psychologist was first mentioned by Ligtner Witmer in 1907 and described as "the study of individuals, by observation or experimentation, with the intention of promoting change." [1] As subfield of psychology, these professionals comprise a large portion of this field of study. By combining the science of psychology with the research of complex human problems they are able to assess and treat an array of psychological and psychiatric problems. They can be found working in various facilities where medical services are provided. Privately, they provide short and long-term outpatient care to individuals who are experiencing psychological problems that inhibit normalcy in their day-to-day activities. Clinical Psychologist are not limited to client services, but also in engage in other areas of treatment including:

- Assessment and diagnosis of psychological

disorders

- Treatment of psychological disorders
- Offering testimony in legal settings
- Teaching
- Conducting research
- Drug and alcohol treatment
- Creating and administering program to treat and prevent social problems

The mental health community for the most part stops short of healing in regard to mental health disorders to using recovery as the wellness terminology. Substance Abuse and Mental Health Services Administration (SAMHSA) defines recovery as: *"A process of change through which individuals improve their health and wellness, live a self-directed life, and strive to reach their full potential"*. (2) SAMHSA believes that this working definition will distinguish advance recovery opportunities for individuals suffering with mental health disorders as well as unify peers, families, funders, and providers on the concepts of recovery. Through the Recovery Support Strategic Initiative, SAMHSA further defines recovery with four major dimensions to consider when assessing the level of recovery. The four dimensions are health, home, purpose and community. In addition to the working definition the committee assigned ten major areas that were agreed upon as the basis for these dimensions. Below are those ten dimensions:

- Hope
- Person-Driven
- Many Pathways
- Holistic
- Peer Support
- Relational
- Culture
- Addresses Trauma
- Strengths/Responsibility
- Respect

The first is **Hope**, and is most critical is the process of recovery. This single area will dictate the access to care and the submission to treatment plans. Hope introduces the concept that a diagnosed individual can overcome the challenges they are confronted with in their struggles with their individual disease.

The next principle is **Person-Driven** and is dependent solely on the individual in treatment. The ability to have the client insert their own goals for life and to construct a path toward these goals is critical to this principle.

The **Many Pathways** principle has a broad array of pathways, but acknowledges that the chosen pathway for each individual is unique. The choice of professional clinical treatment; medications; faith-based support; peer support are all options according to the many pathways. Because mental illness affects the life of an individual completely (mind, body and spirit), it is important to include attention to all these areas in recovery.

Holistic Principle suggest that every area of an individual's life, from medical care to community involvement should be integrated into the recovery process.

Peer Support offers a unique opportunity for the individual/family to realize that others suffer in the same areas, but are operating as productive members of society. It has also been reported that the peer workers, who are also in recovery, find encouragement in helping others. Another principle is knowing that there are others who believe in their ability to recover.

These people make up the **Relational** principle in the 10 Guiding Principles to Recovery. Often these are not family members or past relationships, but rather new ones in the support community who offer a feeling of inclusion and community participation which is vital to recovery.

Culture among those suffering from mental illness is diverse, being able to connect individuals with like race, beliefs and traditions allows the path to recovery more personalized, yielding increased probability of successful treatment.

Another principle is **Addresses Trauma**, which can include physical or sexual abuse, violence on all levels, war and disaster, which is often associated with mental health problems. Opportunities to visit these areas in a safe and comfortable environment enhances overall treatment.

Strengths/Responsibility are both something that should be included in the recovery process. Knowing their own strengths and taking responsibility to speak to those areas with family, clinicians and peers is individually empowering.

And finally **Respect** for the individual is warranted as the decision to come forward is often a difficult one. When these individuals are appreciated it promotes self-acceptance and an overall positive outlook.

Much work has been done in the area of mental health recovery, however there is more observation and research to be done to ensure that the models presented are proven effective. The cry for a culturally diverse population of mental health professionals is a major focus, given culture plays big part in the overall probability of recovery. It is important that individuals can see those that have similar cultural (race, beliefs, values and traditions) backgrounds. Thus there is work to be done in exposing the deficiencies in this area and encouraging individuals of color, various traditions and diverse faith persuasions to consider these professions as a vital career choice.

Spiritual Healing

The previous pages delved into the concept of recovery which in the minds of many is different than healing. These two words are often used interchangeably, but are slightly different depending on the situation. In order to help make the distinction, there must be some consensus of the difference between disease and illness. To simplify both terms when referring to disease, it is referencing the abnormal condition of an organ and illness are the feelings associated with the disease. Note that illness can occur when a disease is not present, because it also involves feelings, moods, beliefs and fears it is a personal experience. Now in reference to the topic, an individual would need a healing to deal with a disease which will be manifested in the recovery from the illness. Recovery simply says that an individual can return to a normalcy that is noted by their status prior to their illness manifesting. This does not imply by any means that the individual is free of any disease or even the disease that facilitated the illness. Then for this writing, healing refers to the supernatural elimination of the disease.

The supernatural healing of diseases is one of those heavily debated subjects. For the most part many people discount or at the least waver at the existence. This debate thickens when the conversation of mental disease/illness is introduced. The two overarching questions are: Does God still heal supernaturally? and Is there a difference between healing of mental illness and physical illness? The answer is a resounding, Yes and No. Yes, there are documented cases of supernatural healing in the 21st century and in reference to supernatural healing, physical illness and mental illness are the same, God heals all sicknesses.

Often it is spoken to individuals suffering with mental illness, pull yourself together. This dialogue is often non-productive as the nature of mental illness often leaves the individual without the ability to bring change. In these instances, the faith community oftentimes likens the illness to a demonic possession. While there is some semblance, the manifestations of a demonic possessed individual and a mentally-ill are blurred, but distinguishable via spiritual discernment. When an individual is not able to bring change within their own power, there are two choices:

- by 'medicine' - the scientific application of things known to heal the things wrong with peoples' bodies: antibiotics, operations, antipsychotics, maybe even therapy.

- by 'healing' - and by this I mean full removal of symptoms not to return and healing of the underlying problem: enacted by the holy spirit.

There are still ongoing debates by professionals in regards to healing, several doctrines that teach against it and ongoing discussion as to how to label supernatural occurrences which is subject only to the individual and his/her experience. This debate continues because what the Bible taught as a normal occurrence has in the 21st century become abnormal. Throughout the Gospels and the book of Acts in the New Testament there are various lessons and examples of healing of illnesses. Furthermore, Jesus commanded His followers in Matthew to heal all sicknesses and diseases. This then settles from the writer's perspective the validity of the availability of supernatural healing.

> *Matthew 10:1 And when he had called unto him his twelve disciples, he gave them power against unclean spirits, to cast them out, and to heal all manner of sickness and all manner of disease. 2*

> *Now the names of the twelve apostles are these;*
> *The first, Simon, who is called Peter, and Andrew*
> *his brother; James the son of Zebedee, and John*
> *his brother; 3 Philip, and Bartholomew; Thomas,*
> *and Matthew the publican; James the son of*
> *Alphaeus, and Lebbaeus, whose surname was*
> *Thaddaeus; 4 Simon the Canaanite, and Judas*
> *Iscariot, who also betrayed him. 5 These twelve*
> *Jesus sent forth, and commanded them, saying, Go*
> *not into the way of the Gentiles, and into any city*
> *of the Samaritans enter ye not: 6 But go rather*
> *to the lost sheep of the house of Israel.*

Additional scriptural texts that speak to New Testament supernatural healing include 1 Corinthians 12 where the gift of healing is listed, John 9:1-3 where Jesus explains that not all sickness is attributed to sin, in Luke 13:32 where He distinguishes casting out demons to healing. As the scriptures are searched, the fall of all mankind in Genesis is the sole source of all sickness and disease. None of which existed at the creation. God's desire has always been to "heal" the broken relationship caused by the fall, but often the inclusion of healing the physical is left out. A writer on the website entitled Mind and Soul, writes the six-fold areas that constitutes holistic healing. Five of these are listed below:

MIND - if we are made in the image of God, we strive towards achieving the mind of Christ.

EMOTIONS - we are in need of inner healing as our souls cry out to God and our past continues to have a hold over us.

PHYSICAL - this is the most obvious and the most tangible. There are many examples of physical healing in the Bible.

SPIRITUAL - there is a link between sin and healing: as we confess our sins we are healed.

SOCIAL - when Jesus healed there is always a social element

Healing Conditions

While God hears our prayers for healing, one must understand there are circumstances that need to be present to ensure the environment/atmosphere is right for God to move. No one is powerful enough to make God move, even in a situation of healing. One of the most obvious conditions that should be present is a belief that healing is part of the New Testament promise. Without faith God cannot move, therefor the prayer of faith according to James in chapter 5 verses 14-16 must be prayed. Without this faith it is more likely that the prayer of faith will not be prayed, human nature dictates that if an individual does not believe he/she is unlikely to pray. Another condition that facilitates the supernatural healing of an individual is the gift of healing. A Christian with this special gift has been gifted for healing in the Body. This doesn't mean that healing cannot take place without such an individual, but because God has placed the gift in the individual the presence of the gift increases the probability of healing, especially when there is a willingness to be healed. And finally, there should be a Grace or the favor of God to heal.

Although it is the will of God for His people to be healed, there will be occasions when healing doesn't take place. Understanding these times will also take a level of faith that says God is Sovereign as recorded in

Deuteronomy 29:29 The secret things belong unto the LORD our God: but those things which are revealed belong unto us and to our children forever, that we may do all the words of this law. As much as the environment is prepared to make it conditionally available, only God can ultimately perform the healing, here is where His grace is needed.

While conditions for healing are necessary, there is no illness that is exempt from the possibility of healing. Because the subject matter of this paper is mental illness, certainly it too is an illness candidate for healing. Nothing about mental illness excludes it from the list, healing is possible. There are those suffering who need to hear that message communicated, especially from the pulpits of their place of worship. The combination of understanding and support breeds hope and hope breeds faith and faith is foundation for healing. Holistic healing is both physical and mental healing. In the case of mental illness this is ever so critical because of the close interwoven connection of the soul and spirit.

Unfortunately, the ministry for the mentally ill is not a normal occurrence in the evangelical faith-based community. All hurting people in the earth should have access to help from Jesus and it is the work of the church to make sure it is available. All too often there is a lack of education surrounding this crucial issue and a willingness to embrace it is absent. Because the love and compassion of Jesus has invaded the life of a Christian that same love and compassion should be in abundance for all that are hurting. The model of this is found in Jesus, when He healed those that were even despised and rejected as seen in *Matthew 9:35, And Jesus went about all the cities and villages, teaching in their synagogues, and preaching the gospel of the kingdom, and healing every sickness and every disease among the people.* Jesus obviously is not prejudice to what kind of health issue an individual is suffering, but it seems the church has gone blind to the needs of broken minds, spirits and bodies to individuals and families with mental illness. Individuals with chronic brain and nervous system issues require many interventions to bring them to the door of recovery and ultimately to complete supernatural healing. Because of the overwhelming need for support, the body of Christ needs to commit to a deeper understanding and open to education to the models of care for the mentally ill.

After all is said the single focus is to enlighten the faith-based community of the need for ministry for a hurting population. Ministry for this group of individuals is intentional, strategic and God inspired. The complexity of the illness typically causes many to shy away, but the overwhelming truth is that God looks for the hard cases. If God is available to assist in tough situations, why would the faith-based community not want to embrace the opportunity to see God work miracles?

Demonization of Mental Illness

Chapter 6

Conclusion of the Matter

This chapter will consolidate the previous research, ideology and theology presented earlier in this book. In an effort to promote *Wholeness in the Church*, the argument to encourage the faith-based community to get involved with individuals and families with mental illness issues, will build from examining the clinical aspects of mental illness to the supernatural power available to heal ***all*** illnesses. The point has been made that the compassion of Jesus is the example that should be followed, as well as reveal the Grace that is available to make a difference.

The Definition

First, mental Illness is not a new term or phenomenon, but as most things in our society, the ideas and perceptions have morphed in various directions over the years. The idea of mental illness continues to find its strength in the individual perception of the term. The perception of the term is critical for the digesting of the material that has been presented throughout the chapters. Without a consistency in the reader's ideas, the receptivity of the thoughts presented could be prematurely rejected or accepted. Therefore, presenting a definition seems necessary in the very beginning.

The word clinical or nonclinical in reference to mental illness seems unnecessary at the onset of hearing the two terms in conjunction to mental illness. The state of being ill, in most cases, has undergone the calisthenics needed to establish the symptoms and signs as part of a diagnosis, but because the symptoms for mental illnesses are often unseen and subject to disclosure of the patient, making the proper diagnosis or any diagnosis becomes difficult in some cases. Webster's dictionary, presents the idea that clinical relates to the interaction and work around real patients in a controlled environment, such as a hospital or clinic. When the signs and/or symptoms align with the outcomes of the specific study, then a person can be properly diagnosed. This diagnosis would then be considered a clinical diagnosis. Throughout this book, the idea of clinical has been assumed in the mention of mental illnesses and behaviors associated to those illnesses.

Diversity in the U.S.

Mental illness in the United States is broad and diverse in the understanding and perception of the disease. The disparity in the perceptions are not simply across cultural boundaries, but research has found that even within cultures there are differences in the idea of mental illness. For instance, American Indian tribes operate with no stigmatism to mental health, other tribes stigmatize some mental illness and other tribes stigmatize any treatment or existence of mental illnesses. Another example is how the Asian American community regards mental illness as a place of shame, as Asians are high on maintaining emotional self-control. In one survey, Chinese Americans were asked to respond to the question, what if one of their children married or reproduced with an individual with various genetic levels of mental illnesses. Opposite of European Americans, Chinese American's unwillingness lessened while the European surveyors had increased numbers in their unwillingness. This clearly exhibits the variations that exist in our country in regard to stigmatization to mental health.

Ethnic groups in America also experience significant differences. When an extensive 18-month observational study was conducted based on an ethnographic study of 25 living with a severe mental illness and also living in the inner city, researchers found that European Americans chose mental health treatment, but African Americans and Latino individuals often cited stigma as the reason for not seeking professional help. In addition, African Americans verbalized a frustration with the introduction of medication and Latinos believed that their social status would ultimately be damaged by such a diagnosis. As late as 2010, 63% of African Americans still viewed a diagnosis of depression a "personal weakness". Many professionals believe that the fact that African Americans are highly reluctant to accept treatment are therefore less likely to receive a proper diagnosis, thus suffering with the illness for longer periods. All of these oddities in cultures within the USA should serve as a reason to improve access to health care.

Perception

The perception of an individual on any subject matter will overwhelmingly drive how a person respond and interact in that particular area. Because statistics reveal that one in four US adult age individuals are diagnosed with a mental disorder in a given year, it is more common than realized. In the case of mental illness, perception will ultimately promote how opportunities and support are provided for the mentally ill. These same perceptions will also reveal how an individual experiences and expresses his/her own emotional and psychological distress and will dictate if they too will seek help in this area. Many adults that suffer with other chronic conditions, such as heart disease, cancer, and epilepsy also experience depression and anxiety. This is important in that a negative perception can interfere with the self-care and diminish an individual's quality of life. This negativity is driven by limited personal knowledge through knowing someone living with mental illness, personal and cultural stereotypes, media, and past restrictions or practices experienced with mental health institutions or health insurance. All too often this negative perception produces avoidance, exploitation and possibly discrimination. On the other hand, if these same individuals could acquire a more positive attitude, the behavior and interactions could be changed and result in more inclusive behaviors, such as dating or hiring an individual with mental illness.

Previously in this text, the phenomena of stigma were introduced. A formal definition of the word has been presented as – a cluster of negative attitudes and beliefs that motivate the general public to fear, reject, avoid, and discriminate against people with mental illnesses (President's New Freedom Commission on Mental Health, p. 4, 2003). Often the premise that all people should be able to function well in regard to employment, education, community and relationships is jeopardized when stigma exists. If a society is able to operate by the stigmas interwoven in the community, this can lead to exclusion or discrimination. While we can examine mental health stigmatization as an isolated area, unfortunately we see the residue of these negative perceptions bleeding into our communities. Just for an example, the diminished quality of life is evident when an individual with untreated mental illness is unable to find gainful employment that provide for his/her basic needs. Included in this absence of needs is access to health care, which further presents more negative outcomes. These individual are basically living in poverty and acquire other social disadvantages which interfere with healthy self-esteem and further compounds the symptoms of mental illness. This is often debilitating for individuals and subsequently presents a challenge to prevention efforts in the mental health community.

Religious Perception

In the last several decades, scientific research has been done and presented to the public in medical and psychological journals. This material has helped in religious organizations revisiting traditional doctrines that exclude involvement with the mental health community. This course of action has become favorable and has fostered the trend of mental health professionals seeking an understanding of how religious involvement in mature adults affects both medical and mental well-being. The outcome to this trending is a more compassionate approach to the care plan of the individual.

Unfortunately, there is plenty of documentation that outlines the negative experiences individuals suffering with mental illness receive from church leaders and/or the religious community. Often the rhetoric of acceptance is conveyed, but individuals suffering have reported that acceptance was not given. In a study released by Lifeway Research, an evangelical research organization, they stated although many seek help from their church community, they most likely will not receive help on Sunday mornings. The study revealed that most Protestant senior pastors (66 percent) seldom speak to their congregation about mental illness.

Treatment Disparity

In an attempt to access treatment, on the system-level, families are faced with trying to combine their access to the health care system and the mental health systems simultaneously. Aligning the medical issues with the disorders hampers what medical professionals call coordination of services. As noted previously, the existence of comorbidities is extremely possible with a seriously mentally ill patient. When the gap between the two health services are widened, specialized care is hindered. The hindrances include, but is not limited to finding specialized care, lack of transportation and simply cost.

On the provider-level the overwhelming concern is the lack of training among the providers to deal to with the different medical/mental conditions. It is not uncommon for the mental health professional to lack training for the medical issues of the patient and vice-versa. The provider-level barriers are also seen in the patient's apprehension to treatment based on pass stigmas they experienced with their provider. These include both medical and mental providers. While it is commonly accepted that medical providers are less compassionate, it is also true that some mental health providers also lack empathy. And most importantly, many believe individual-level hindrances are the hardest to overcome. The litany of barriers in this area is as unique as the individuals that report this area as a hindrance. They range from mistrust of providers, as mentioned above to the inability to navigate the process to access care based on the cultural, language and educational challenges. Ultimately, the merging of both systems can produce meaningful results.

Infirmities

Researching infirmities, the King James Version of the bible will be utilized for all scriptural text references as well as any tools for exegesis. Strong's accordance lists the first mention of the word infirmity in Hebrew as *davah* and is found in **Leviticus 12:2**. The Hebrew meaning is to be ill, be unwell. Infirmity, in Greek is *astheneia* and is first found in **Luke 13:11** and is interpreted feebleness (of mind or body). The English word asthenia has for its root the same Greek word and according to Webster means lack or loss of strength. These are key to how the Bible project the idea of infirmity/illness. There is a pattern in scripture that reverts to first mentioned and expands on the biblical perspective throughout the Bible. As we build the case for mental wholeness, this is the foundation from which the building begins.

Proper study of the Bible should include contextual reference. Extracting a single verse can often lead to misinterpretation of the thought being conveyed. The Old Testament scripture in **Leviticus 12:2**, looking at verses 1 through 7 gives a complete thought surrounding the text. The infirmity mentioned here is associated to a woman's condition after she has given birth to a child. Two points are critical here; she is considered ill and anyone that approaches her would also be considered ill. This Old Testament teaching perpetuated the idea that the natural process of a woman's childbirth experience is similar to an illness. There are countless speculations as to why she was considered unclean, but for this book, investigating those possibilities are beyond the scope. Many believe that the uncleanliness of a Mother after seven days for a boy and 14 days for a girl, although a sin offering was required, was not eluding to sin. This may be the case, from a biblical historical perspective, but overall speculations cannot be made. Then the text in **Luke 13:11** is housed within the contextual reference of Luke chapter 13 verses 6 through 11. The infirmity mentioned here is clearly a physical one and has caused significant grief for a long period of time. Unlike the previous text there is clearly a compassion that is exuded for this woman because of her illness. Given they are both what the Bible says are infirmities the response to each is totally different. The first inclination is to try and understand the difference between the two, which is simply time.

An attempt to totally understand the minute specifics of the time is not necessary for this writing. While the teachings of the time may not be understood, what is understood today is that society has evolved from at least the behavior associated with the Leviticus text. The majority of people in the 21st century would think it absurd to shun a mother for a week after her giving birth. Removing the tradition of this behavior has provided for numerous positives in assisting a woman during a time that her physical, mental and emotional faculties are experiencing noticeable change. These are two examples of how change can be positively affective, there are countless of other examples that reflect progression of mindsets and behaviors evolving as a result of progression in society. Oddly, from statistical analysis, it is reported that mental illness has not experienced the same luxury of progressive thinking. Perhaps the ability to categorize mental health disorders in the disease category is what hinders the progression. Moving society to a new paradigm requires extensive education for the religious community. Often this is a difficult task as the perception is that the progression is in violation of doctrine, dogma or ritualistic customs of the organization.

Traditionalism

The church has operated so long in traditionalism as it pertains to the archaic teaching around mental health although the mention of mental illness and demon possession is recorded in the Bible and makes a clear distinction between the two. For instance, in the New Testament **Mark 5:1-16** and **Luke 8:26-37**, Jesus encounters a man the Bible clearly identifies as one that was possessed. There are several similarities in the actions of this man as in one that is mentally unstable, but in addition to those areas he displayed supernatural spiritual power. For instance:

- The demons had supernatural power to break the chains
- The demons knew who Jesus was before He approached him
- The demons knew that Jesus was the Messiah
- The demons were causing the man to speak.

This wasn't the first time Jesus encountered a demon. In **Mark 1:32-34** and **Luke 4:33-36**. So clearly there is record of demon possession, but there is also record of mental illness. If scripture will take care in the making the distinction, the ability to understand the difference is revealed in the Word for all to know. In **Deuteronomy 28:27-29**, **1 Samuel 21:12-15**, **Mark 3:20-21** and **Acts 26:24-25**. The record in Deuteronomy interprets the Hebrew word for insane as madness in verse number 28. See the scripture below in context:

> ***Deuteronomy 28:28*** *The LORD shall smite thee with madness, and blindness, and astonishment of heart*

These infirmities and many like these continue to plague mankind. The understanding of the divine design of man from creation is necessary. God made man a tripartite being from the beginning. The ideal biblical text that this writing will use for the basis for the trichotomy of man is displayed in **1Thessalonians 5:23**. Here the writer conveys the two distinct immaterial parts of the human nature. Below is this scripture within context.

> ***1 Thessalonians 5:23*** *And the very God of peace sanctify you wholly; and I pray God your whole*

spirit and soul and body be preserved blameless unto the coming of our Lord Jesus Christ.

The first part of the trichotomy referenced in the text is spirit or the Greek word pneuma, which is translated as spirit in the scriptures 111 times and Holy Ghost more than 85 times. This is the part of mankind that desires to know God and seeks to delight Him. Only this part of the human nature has any knowledge of those things in the spirit or that which is spiritual. Therefore, it is believed that it is this part of the human nature that has to be reborn as it has taken on the nature of sinful flesh at birth. This point is crucial in understanding the soul(mind) because of the interwoven closeness of these two entities it is not unthinkable that one effects the other. The health of the spirit can dictate the health of the soul(mind) or vice-versa.

The second part of the trichotomy referenced in **1Thessalonians 5:23** is soul or the Greek word psyche, which is where we get our English words psychology, psychiatrist and psyche. Although this same Greek word is translated with multiple definitions throughout the scriptures, the thought in this text is to introduce the trichotomy of man. Because spirit and soul are often used interchangeably and we find both here, the assumption is that the writer is making a distinction. Some theologians believe that the struggle experienced is the fight for control of the soul by the flesh and the spirit. Assuming the spirit has been transformed to be in relationship with God the conflict with the flesh is immediate as the same transformation has not taken place. The flesh still houses the desires to live destructively and operate with negative persuasion, but the spirit thrives for the complete opposite. The mind now operates as the control center for behavior and can be influenced by the spirit or the flesh. Thus, writers of the New Testament letter often make references to the battle that will continuously exist for mankind in the earth realm. The behavior manifestation is the result of which voice – flesh or spirit – the mind yielded to at the time. This analogy so closely resembles the activity of an individual that suffering with a mental health diagnosis such as schizophrenia. The battle to decide which voice to listen just became more intense as more voices are introduced. The mind then has a tremendous responsibility of remaining well. Some theologians believe the mind is the center of all things and have isolated 3 key categories that the activity of the mind can be categorized into; volition/will, intellect/reason and emotion/feeling.

The third and final part of the trichotomy referenced is body or the Greek word sōma, which is translated body over 144 times in the Bible. The more obvious of the three areas of mankind is this area. Clearly this word references the outer part of an individual which houses the other two areas. While often in scripture text this same word is translated sinful nature, this eludes to the theological premise that what is hidden in the flesh is this nature that is contrary to the things of God. The recanting of the creation, introduces the "dirtiness" of flesh in **Genesis 2:7**. Researchers have found that the same elements that are found in soil are also found in the human body. With this as a backdrop, it is no wonder there's a need for the spirit to be changed in order to combat the mind.

The soul interwoven with the spirit and flesh presents the ultimate problem for the mentally ill, but after all is said the single focus is to enlighten the faith-based community of the need for ministry for a hurting population. Ministry for this group of individuals is intentional, strategic and God inspired. The complexity of the illness, typically causes many to shy away, but the overwhelming truth is that God looks for the hard cases.

Demonization of Mental Illness

Bibliography

About (2016). "Mind, Body, Spirit" Retrieved April 20, 2016 from http://healing.about.com/od/healthyliving/u/mindbodyspirit.htm

Alexander, Taylor (2012). *mental health: a friend, a home, a job*, Retrieved April 15, 2016 from http://ontario.cmha.ca/files/2012/07/olm_stigma_matters_200902.pdf

American Psychological Association (2014). Ethnic Minorities Still Receiving Inferior Mental Health Treatment, Says APA Journal, Retrieved April 18, 2016 from http://www.apa.org/news/press/releases/2014/12/inferior-treatment.aspx

Behere, Prakash B. et al (2013). *Religion and mental health*, Retrieved April 15, 2016, from http://www.ncbi.nlm.nih.gov/pmc/articles/PMC3705681/

Blue Letter Bible Online, Retrieved April 18, 2016 from https://www.blueletterbible.org/

Bible Study Tools (2014). Retrieved April 2016 from http://www.biblestudytools.com/

Binder, Renee (2015). *Working to Decriminalize Mental Illness*, Retrieved April 18 2016, from https://psychiatry.org/news-room/apa-blogs/apa-blog/2015/10/working-to-decriminalize-mental-illness

Brain World (2014). *Millennial Mental Health*, Retrieved April 18, 2016 from http://brainworldmagazine.com/millennial-mental-health/

Brekke, John S. et al (2013). *Reducing Health Disparities for People with Serious Mental Illness: Development and Feasibility of a Peer Health Navigation Intervention*, Retrieved April 18, 2016 from http://www.healthnavigation.org/files/docs/2013-04-26_Reducing-Health-Disparities-For-People-With-Serious-Mental-Illness.pdf

Caddell, Jenev (2016). *What Is a Psychotherapist?*, Retrieved April 15, 2016 from http://mentalhealth.about.com/od/psychotherapy/fl/What-is-a-psychotherapist.htm

Centers for Disease Control and Prevention (2016). *Mental Illness*, Retrieved April 15, 2016 from http://www.cdc.gov/mentalhealth/basics/mental-illness.htm

Centers for Disease Control and Prevention (2012). *Attitudes Toward Mental Illness*, Retrieved April 15, 2016 from http://www.cdc.gov/hrqol/Mental_Health_Reports/pdf/BRFSS_Full%20Report.pdf

Cherry, Kendra (2016). *What Is the Diagnostic and Statistical Manual (DSM)?*, Retrieved April 15, 2016 from https://www.verywell.com/the-diagnostic-and-statistical-manual-dsm-2795758

Cherry, Kendra (2016). *What Is Clinical Psychology?*, Retrieved April 20, 2016 from https://www.verywell.com/what-is-clinical-psychology-2795000

Citizens Commission on Human Rights International (2016). *REAL DISEASE VS. MENTAL "DISORDER"*, Retrieved April 15, 2016 from http://www.cchr.org/quick-facts/real-disease-vs-mental-disorder.html

Emma of Believer's Brain (2012). *Demons and Mental Illness,* Retrieved April 18 2016, from https://believersbrain.com/2012/11/29/demons-and-mental-illness/

Etkin, Amit (2015). *Scientists seek to map origins of mental illness, develop noninvasive treatment*, Retrieved April 15, 2016 from https://med.stanford.edu/news/all-news/2015/01/scientists-seek-to-map-origins-of-mental-illness.html

Faith and Health Connection (2016). *Spirit, Soul and Body – How God Designed Us*, Retrieved April 20, 2016 from http://www.faithandhealthconnection.org/the_connection/spirit-soul-and-body/

Goebert, Deborah (2014). *Cultural Disparities in Mental Health Care: Closing the Gap*, Retrieved April 18, 2016 from http://www.psychiatrictimes.com/cultural-psychiatry/cultural-disparities-mental-health-care-closing-gap

Greenstein, Laura (2015). *9 Ways to Fight Mental Health Stigma,* Retrieved April 15, 2016 from https://www.nami.org/Blogs/NAMI-Blog/October-2015/9-Ways-to-Fight-Mental-Health-Stigma#sthash.gSGZPy4n.dpuf

Hell Hades and the Afterlife (2014). *Understanding Human Nature: Spirit, Mind & Body*, Retrieved April 20, 2016 from http://www.hellhadesafterlife.com/hell/mind-body-spirit

Izumi, Lance T. et al (1996). *Corrections, Criminal Justice, and the Mentally Ill:*

Some Observations About Costs, Retrieved April 18 2016, from http://www.mhac.org/pdf/PacificResearchStudy.pdf

Jongbloed, Andrea (2014). *4 Misconceptions About Mental Illness and Faith,* Retrieved April 15, 2016 from http://www.relevantmagazine.com/god/church/4-misconceptions-about-mental-illness-and-faith

Lerner-Wren, Ginger (2014). *The Criminalization of*

the Mentally Ill in America — Have We Reached a Flashpoint?, Retrieved April 18 2016, from http://www.huffingtonpost.com/ginger-lernerwren/the-criminalization-of-th_b_5607820.html

Lifeway Research (2014). *Study of Acute Mental Illness and Christian Faith*, Retrieved April 15, 2016 from http://lifewayresearch.com/wp-content/uploads/2014/09/Acute-Mental-Illness-and-Christian-Faith-Research-Report-1.pdf

Manderscheid, Ronald W. et al (2009). *Evolving Definitions of Mental Illness and Wellness*, Retrieved April 15, 2016 from http://www.ncbi.nlm.nih.gov/pmc/articles/PMC2811514/

Martin, The Rev. James (2015). *Why are some Catholics so afraid of change?*, Retrieved April 18, 2016 from http://www.cnn.com/2015/10/26/world/catholics-fear-change/index.html

Mayo Clinic Staff (2016). *Mental illness: Definition*, Retrieved April 15, 2016 from http://www.mayoclinic.org/diseases-conditions/mental-illness/basics/definition/con-20033813

Mental Health America (2016). *About Mental Health America*, Retrieved April 15, 2016 from http://www.mentalhealthamerica.net/about-us

Mental Health Foundation (2016). *Recovery*, Retrieved April 18, 2016 from https://www.mentalhealth.org.uk/a-to-z/r/recovery

Merriam-Webster Online, Retrieved April 15, 2016 from

http://www.merriam-webster.com/dictionary

Messiah's House of Yahvah (2016). *Demon Possession vs. Mental Illness*, Retrieved April 18 2016, from http://messiahshouseofyahvah.org/ArticlesAndMore/DemonPossession.V.MentalIllness.html

Miranda, Jeanne et al (2008). *Mental Health in the Context of Health Disparities*, Retrieved April 18, 2016 from http://ajp.psychiatryonline.org/doi/pdf/10.1176/appi.ajp.2008.08030333

Murashko, Alex (2014). *Stigma of Mental Illness 'Still Real' Inside the Church, LifeWay Research Reveals*, Retrieved April 15, 2016 from http://www.christianpost.com/news/stigma-of-mental-illness-still-real-inside-the-church-lifeway-research-reveals-126832/

NAMI (2016). *Mental Health Conditions*, Retrieved April 15, 2016 from https://www.nami.org/Learn-More/Mental-Health-Conditions

Nordqvist, Christian (2015). *Public Health Mental Health What Is Health? What Does Good Health Mean?*, Retrieved April 20, 2016 from

http://www.medicalnewstoday.com/articles/150999.
php

Schumaker, Erin (2015). *It's Time To Stop Using These Phrases When It Comes To Mental Illness*, Retrieved April 15, 2016 from http://www.huffingtonpost.com/2015/04/17/mental-illness-vocabulary_n_7078984.html

Stanford, Matthew S., McAlister, Kandace R (2008). *Perception of Serious Mental Illness in the Church*, Retrieved April 15, 2016 from http://www.baylorisr.org/wp-content/uploads/stanford_perceptions.pdf

State of Connecticut (2016). *MENTAL HEALTH: CULTURE, RACE, AND ETHNICITY*, Retrieved April 18, 2016 from http://www.ct.gov/dmhas/lib/dmhas/publications/mhethnicity.pdf

Stetzer, Ed (2013). *Mental Illness and the Church: New Research on Mental Health from LifeWay Research*, Retrieved April 18, 2016 from http://www.christianitytoday.com/edstetzer/2013/september/mental-illness-and-church-new-research-on-mental-health-fro.html

Substance Abuse and Mental Health Services Administration (2012). *SAMHSA's*

Working Definition of Recovery, Retrieved April 20, 2016 from http://store.samhsa.gov/shin/content/PEP12-RECDEF/PEP12-RECDEF.pdf

Substance Abuse and Mental Health Services Administration Ad Council (2016). *What a Difference a Friend Makes*, Retrieved April 15, 2016 from http://www.mhaac.org/uploads/documents/What%20A%20Difference-ENG.pdf

UNITE FOR SIGHT (2012). *Module 2: A Brief History of Mental Illness and the U.S. Mental Health Care System*, Retrieved April 18 2016, from http://www.uniteforsight.org/mental-health/module2

UNITE FOR SIGHT (2012). *Module 3: Priority Mental Health Conditions*, Retrieved April 15, 2016 from http://www.uniteforsight.org/mental-health/module3

UNITE FOR SIGHT (2012). *Module 6: Barriers to Mental Health Care*, Retrieved April 15, 2016 from http://www.uniteforsight.org/mental-health/module6

Waller, Rob (2011). *Healing and Mental Illness*, Retrieved April 20, 2016 from http://www.mindandsoul.info/Articles/238046/Mind_and_Soul/Resources/Healing_and_Mental.aspx

RESOURCES FOR HELP:

Mental Health Emergency Crisis please dial 911

Mental health reseources in your area:

National Suicide Prevention Lifeline: 1-800-273-TALK(8255)
www.suicidepreventionlifeline.org

800-SUICIDE (800-784-2433)

www.findtreatment.samhsa.gov
Anywhere in the country, just enter the address and zip code to get a list of local providers.

Contact Dr. Donna M. Scott for speaking engagements/training/seminars/workshops at:

Donna@UnmaskingSuicide.org
www.unmaskingsuicide.org
Phone/Fax: 1-877-600-1028